Rain Forest Vacation

Margaret Fetty

Rigby®

A Harcourt Achieve Imprint

www.Rigby.com
1-800-531-5015

June 3, 2006

When the school bell rings at 3:30 today, it will mean the beginning of summer vacation. FINALLY! I love school, but I can hardly wait to take off on our trip tomorrow. Mom and I are going to visit the Amazon rain forest in Brazil. Mom will be searching for new types of plants in the rain forest. She's a botanist, which is a scientist who studies plants. Maybe someday I'll grow up to be a botanist like Mom.

CENTRAL AMERICA

ATLANTIC OCEAN

AMAZON RAIN FOREST

BRAZIL

PACIFIC OCEAN

SOUTH AMERICA

N W E S

We studied rain forests in school this year, and I was amazed to find out how many plants and animals, including the jaguar, call the rain forest home. Since I get to actually visit the rain forests of Brazil with Mom, I hope to see some interesting wildlife!

I hope to see a jaguar in the rain forest!

June 4, 2006

It's been a long trip, but we're finally flying over Brazil. I had expected to see endless areas of dark green where the rain forests grow, but instead there are huge patches of brown dirt and light-green grasses. These patches don't have any trees at all!

Mom explained that the rain forests in Brazil are being destroyed by logging companies that are cutting down trees to use for building materials, furniture, and paper. Mining companies are also clearing land so they can mine for underground minerals. Even the native people are clearing giant areas to make cattle ranches and plantations.

Mom showed me this time line that shows how much of the rain forest has been lost to deforestation, or the clearing of trees. In 10 years, Brazil has lost 10,088 square miles of rain forest!

Rain Forest Loss in Brazil

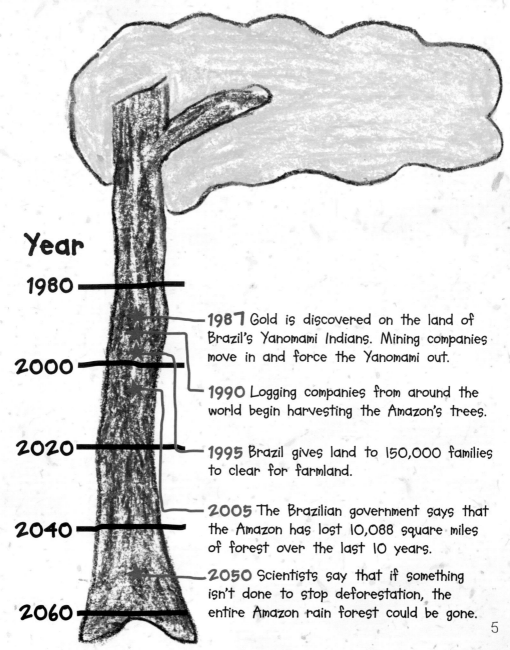

Year

1980

2000

2020

2040

2060

1987 Gold is discovered on the land of Brazil's Yanomami Indians. Mining companies move in and force the Yanomami out.

1990 Logging companies from around the world begin harvesting the Amazon's trees.

1995 Brazil gives land to 150,000 families to clear for farmland.

2005 The Brazilian government says that the Amazon has lost 10,088 square miles of forest over the last 10 years.

2050 Scientists say that if something isn't done to stop deforestation, the entire Amazon rain forest could be gone.

June 18, 2006

   After spending several days in the city of Manaus, Mom and I traveled to the nature preserve and lodge where we'll be staying. We rode in a dugout canoe made from a huge tree trunk. We had to float down the Amazon River because there are only a few roads in the rain forest.

   I knew the trees would be really tall, but I wasn't prepared for these giants!

 The canoes we took to the nature preserve were carved out of huge tree trunks.

My mom pointed out the emergent trees that grow up to 200 feet tall. Emergent trees are the tallest trees in the rain forest. This top layer of forest gets the most sunlight and rain.

Mom said the second layer is the canopy. Most of these trees get lots of sun and grow from 80 to 130 feet tall.

The third layer is the understory, where it is hot and humid. Small trees, flowers, and vines grow there. The bottom layer is the forest floor, which has ferns, dead trees, and fallen leaves.

I can't wait to start exploring!

The Layers of the Rain Forest

Emergent Layer

Canopy

Understory

Forest Floor

June 19, 2006

    I awoke today to whistles, chirps, howls, and screeches. The rain forest animals had already begun their day, and I was missing out! Since Mom was in a meeting, I decided to explore the grounds around the lodge. I hoped that today would be the day I saw my jaguar!

The Amazon rain forest stretches across nine countries and is home to many different types of animals. I love this picture of the colorful parrots!

There are so many different kinds of flowers growing around the buildings. As I bent down to look at a white orchid, a butterfly darted away. I didn't notice the butterfly at first because its wings were transparent—I could see right through them!

The butterfly flew to another flower, kicking up a cloud of pollen. After it had taken a sip of nectar, it flew to another flower. My mom later explained that the butterfly was spreading pollen that would grow new plants. No wonder there are so many flowers around the lodge!

June 21, 2006

Mom had another meeting today. I must have looked disappointed that she couldn't go out with me because she took me to meet Mr. Romel, one of the preserve's guides. Even though it was raining, he offered to take me into the rain forest. Mr. Romel grew up here, so he knows a lot about the plants and animals.

As we hiked along the dark path, Mr. Romel told me about the birds and insects we saw. There were no signs of a jaguar, but the leaf cutter ants were fun to watch.

These insects chew off pieces of leaves, then carry them back to the anthill. Smaller ants, called hitchhikers, ride on top of the leaves and keep the flies away. The leaf cutter ants don't eat these leaves. They use them to grow a fungus that they eat.

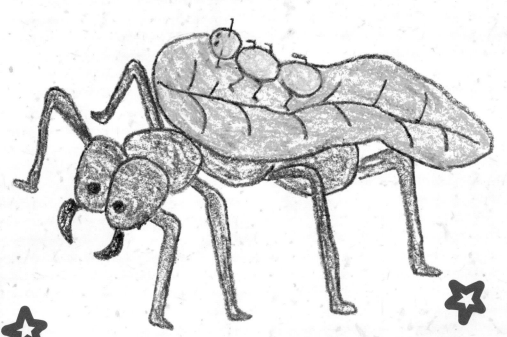

The leaf cutter ant carries the hitchhiker ant on its back. They make a pretty good team!

July 2, 2006

Mr. Romel took Mom and me out to explore the deep parts of the rain forest today, and we hadn't gone far before we heard loud hoots and howls. Mr. Romel said that red howler monkeys always make that loud noise when another animal enters their territory.

As we got closer, I could see a whole group of reddish-brown monkeys high in the canopy. They walked from tree to tree using all four feet. One howler monkey hung from its tail as it ate some leaves.

Howler monkeys are loud enough to be heard eight miles away. Now that's loud!

12

Mr. Romel seemed glad to see the red howlers. He explained that he had not seen many lately because a logging company had chopped down a huge area of trees, destroying their homes. As a result, the monkeys had fewer places to find fruits and flowers to eat. It made me sad to think that these noisy animals might not have enough food.

P.S. Still no jaguar!

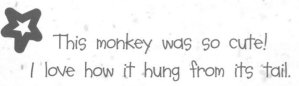
This monkey was so cute! I love how it hung from its tail.

July 10, 2006

Today Mom went to look at bromeliads. These plants have stiff, colorful leaves. While Mom took photographs and made notes, I wandered around looking for jaguar tracks. There were bromeliads everywhere—growing in the soil and on rocks. Some even grew on tree branches. When I took a closer look inside one of them, I found a tiny frog sitting in some water! How cool is that!

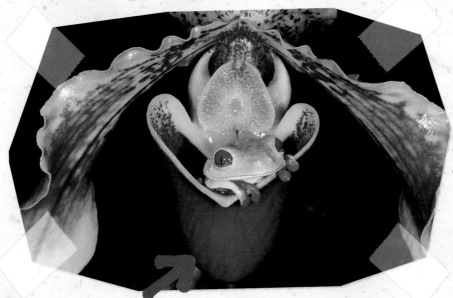

 This tiny frog I found sitting in a bromeliad is a poison dart frog. Its skin is poisonous!

Mom told me that bromeliads could make up their own ecosystem. An ecosystem is a community of plants and animals that live together in an area. In the bromeliad ecosystem, small leaves fall into the water and cause algae to grow. Then mosquitoes come to eat the algae and lay eggs in the water. Before long other small animals, like frogs and lizards, come to live in the bromeliad. I'm amazed at how one plant can be important to so many other rain forest creatures!

Lots of small creatures use the bromeliad for shelter and growing food.

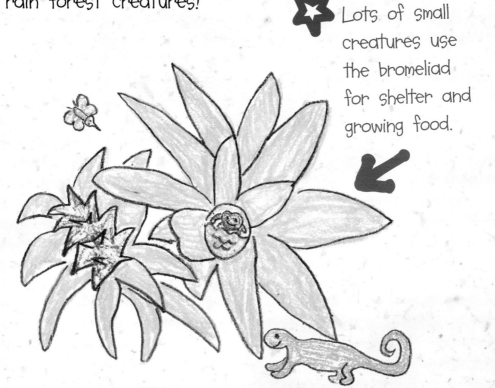

July 15, 2006

Today we began a five-day eco-tour along the Amazon River. Mom says these tours are a great way for the local people to earn money, and it's a way to educate the tourists about the importance of the rain forest. The tour certainly educated me!

We paddled down the Amazon River, and even though it rained hard today, we watched the wildlife come and go from tree to tree.

When I started complaining about the daily rain showers, Mom reminded me that rain kept the rivers full and flowing, which is how many people travel in the rain forest. The rain just takes getting used to.

After the rain stopped, it got really hot. A nice swim would have been a great way to cool off, but I quickly changed my mind when I saw a caiman—a kind of crocodile—lying on the riverbank. So much for swimming to cool off!

July 17, 2006

Today as we started out on our tour, I heard loud squawking from parrots flying above us. When I looked up, I saw huge clouds of smoke rising in the distance. The rain forest was on fire!

Mr. Romel said people were making way for a plantation. Natives used to burn small patches of forest, then after a few years, they'd grow crops there. When they'd moved on to other areas, the old area grew back healthier than before. Today farmers do the same thing. They burn large areas of land. After growing crops for a few years, farmers' cattle graze on the grass. The grass doesn't last, though, and more land is burned for farming.

Parrots and other beautiful birds make their homes in the rain forest's trees. Where will they go when the trees are burned for farming?

Later Mr. Romel pointed to some land that had once been a plantation. He explained that because there were no trees to hold the soil in place, water erosion had carved deep trenches in the soil. Water erosion is when water washes the soil away. I wonder if these people knew that what they were doing to make a living was harming the rain forest.

Forest Fires in Brazil's Amazon Rain Forest

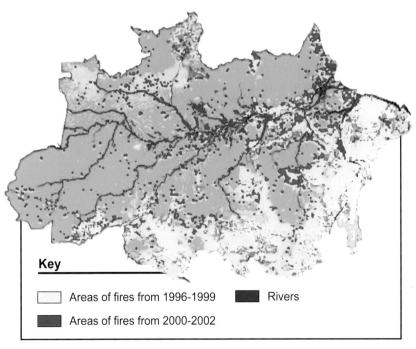

Key

☐ Areas of fires from 1996-1999   ■ Rivers

■ Areas of fires from 2000-2002

July 31, 2006

   I love chocolate, so today was a treat when we got to tour a cacao tree farm. Cacao beans are what chocolate is made from. There's a lot they have to do to turn these beans into sweet chocolate, but visiting the farm was still interesting. I didn't even mind walking an hour in the rain to get there.

Chocolate is sweet, but cacao beans are bitter! Yuck!

On the tour I learned that farmers plant cacao trees in the understory after they thin the canopy. These trees can grow more than 25 feet tall. Wow!★

Workers break open the cacao pods to harvest the beans. This is a great way for the people of Brazil to earn money without harming the rain forest. Plus, there will always be a need for more cacao beans. I mean, who doesn't love chocolate?

I ♥ chocolate!!

P.S. On the way back to the lodge, Mr. Romel pointed to some jaguar tracks in the mud. Now I know there's a jaguar nearby. How exciting!

August 3, 2006

Today when I was out in the forest with Mom, we saw a man picking up a bunch of grapefruit-sized pods off the ground and breaking them open. We stopped to see what he had in his hands, and Mom told me the man was harvesting nuts from the brazil-nut tree. She told me that this, too, was an important moneymaking crop for the country.

The brazil nut grows inside a hard shell similar to a coconut shell.

Mom explained how important the brazil-nut tree is to the rain forest ecosystem. She said that bats spread pollen to the flowers, and many animals eat the nuts for food. New trees grow because animals bury the seeds in the ground.

An agouti looks like a big rat without a tail. It eats brazil nuts.

August 8, 2006

It's always noisy in the forest during the day, but there are also lots of sounds at night, too. Last night I heard hoots, chirps, and croaks.

Mr. Romel took Mom and me on a hike at dusk to check out those sounds. I was so excited because I know jaguars hunt at night, and since I had seen tracks in the area, I kept my fingers crossed that we'd get a glimpse of this shy cat.

 The tapir is a pig-like animal that has a trunk and who eats at night. He loves leaves!

At first we walked with our flashlights on, but then we turned them off. That was a bit scary, especially when we flashed the lights on again and saw the glowing eyes of an owl monkey.

Soon it was time to head back to the lodge. As we walked back, I heard a growl that made my heart jump. It was a jaguar! At least I thought it was. It was too dark to see clearly, and before I could shine my flashlight, the creature was gone.

The owl monkey catches flying moths right out of the air.

I almost saw a jaguar, but it ran away before I could shine my flashlight on it.

25

Mom looked at more plants today, and I helped by taking pictures of the most interesting ones. We lost track of time, and suddenly the sun was setting. As we packed up for the day, Mom froze. In the canopy above was a 10-foot-long boa constrictor! My heart beat wildly as we backed away very slowly. Once we were safely away, I saw a lump in the snake—I guess it had already found dinner!

Boas hunt at night. They wrap around their prey and squeeze it to death.

Some poor animal had been the boa's meal! Mom reminded me that there are many food chains in the rain forest. A food chain shows how living things get their food. Animals eat plants, and then other animals eat the plant eaters. And larger animals eat the meat eaters.

I know that each part of the food chain is important to the survival of the others. If just one plant or animal were to be destroyed, the whole food chain would be affected.

In this food chain, insects eat leaves, then frogs eat the insects, and finally snakes eat the frogs.

August 16, 2006

YUCK—beetles! They crawl all over the forest floor, so there's no telling how many of these insects I've stepped on since I've been here. Mr. Romel told me how important they are to the ecosystem because they help leaves and trees decay. The beetle's wings are hidden beneath a hard shell. They also come in lots of colors. There are so many different types of beetles that scientists still haven't discovered them all.

The rhinoceros dung beetle is especially interesting. It is one of the largest beetles around. The male has horns on its head, much like a rhino. Mr. Romel said the female lays eggs on fresh animal droppings. The droppings become food that the newly hatched beetles eat. Nothing is wasted in the rain forest!

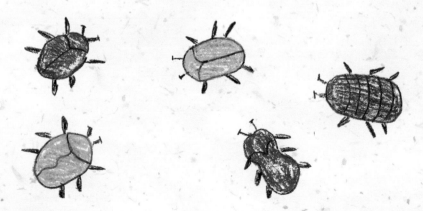

I know how this beetle got its name! That horn looks a lot like a rhino's horn!

August 24, 2006

Exciting news! Mom thinks she's found a new type of plant, so she asked some of the native people if they had ever seen it or used it as a medicine. Mom says that many rain forest plants are used to cure some illnesses.

I remember Mom pointing out a tree called the cinchona. Some people gather the bark from this tree and sell it to companies that make drugs used to fight malaria, a disease that can be deadly.

Mom's new plant has large leaves and a cool yellow flower

I'm so proud of Mom. Scientists like her work to find new plant life that might be able to help people cure horrible illnesses. It's cool to think that Mom may have discovered a plant that could cure a disease!

Mom says that one-and-one-half acres of forest are cut down each second. That's the size of a football field— gone in the blink of an eye!

August 22, 2006

We leave Brazil tomorrow. I never saw my jaguar, but I guess I'm not surprised. The jaguar is an endangered species, which means that there aren't many left. People rarely see them anymore. Natives hunt them for food and for the money they make by selling the skins.

While I think this is wrong, I have some hope, not only for the jaguar, but for the entire rain forest ecosystem. There are lots of people working to save the rain forest because they understand its importance to the world. They have a dream of helping the rain forest and its creatures survive.